紅斗篷經歷過那次兇惡豺狼的
可怕遭遇後，正在花園內嬉戲。
「紅斗篷，」她的媽媽叫道，
「我造了一些甜餅，快來吃呀，
不如拿一些給爸爸，好嗎？」
紅斗篷依然感到有點緊張不安，
不敢進入樹林，但媽媽需要她的幫忙，
爸爸又愛吃甜餅，於是她便答應走一趟。

Red Riding Hood was playing in the garden after her terrible ordeal
with that nasty wolf.
"Red Riding Hood," called her Mum, "I've made cookies, come and get one.
Why not take some to Dad?"
Now Red Riding Hood still felt a bit nervous about going into the wood. But
Mum needed her help, and Dad loved his cookies. So, she agreed to go.

Her Mum counted ten freshly made cookies into a basket. 2, 4, 6, 8, 10.
Red Riding Hood gave her Mum a big hug and off she went.

媽媽數了十個新鮮造好的甜餅，放進籃子去。
二，四，六，八，十。
紅斗篷擁抱媽媽一下後便啓程去了。

她走得不遠便聽到一股細小的聲音：
「紅斗篷，紅斗篷，你有食物嗎？我被困在這塔上已很久了，我真的很飢餓啊。」
「將你的籃子放下來，」紅斗篷說，「我有新鮮美味的甜餅給你。」

She hadn't gone far when she heard a small voice: "Red Riding Hood, Red Riding Hood, have you any food? I've been stuck up in this tower for ages and I'm starving."
"Send down your basket," said Red Riding Hood. "I have a delicious, freshly made cookie for you."

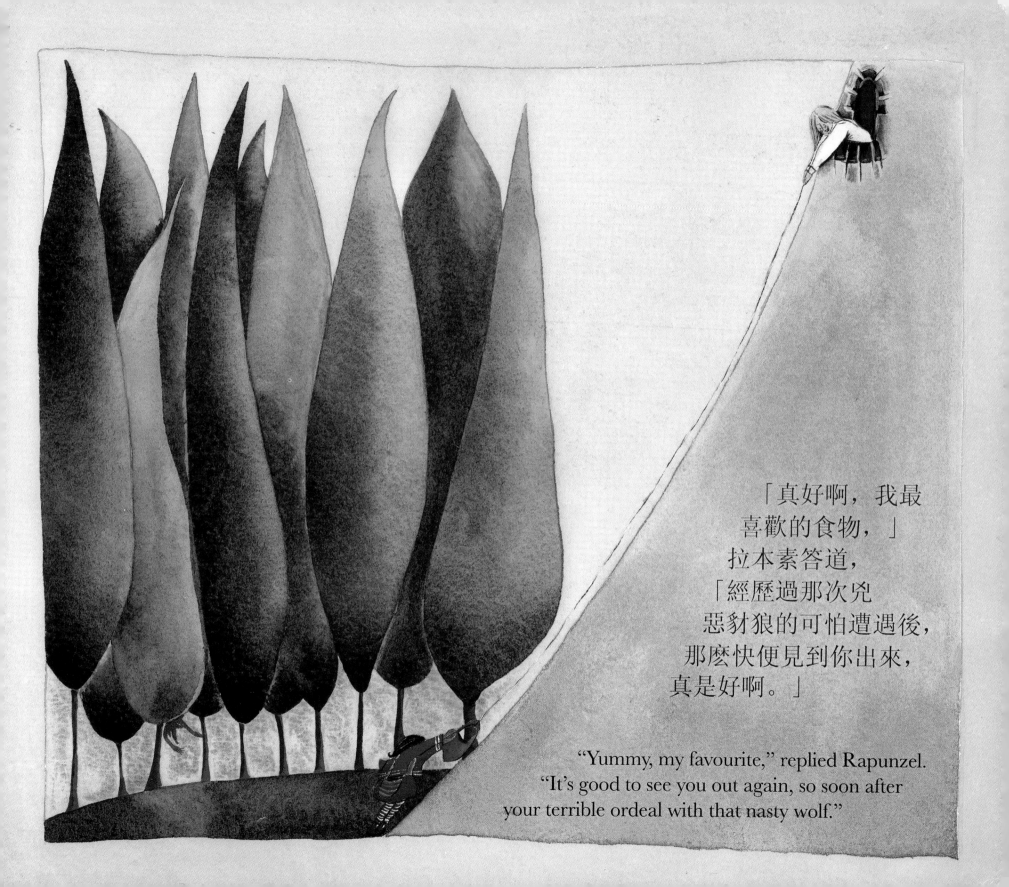

「真好啊，我最
喜歡的食物，」
拉本素答道，
「經歷過那次兇
惡豺狼的可怕遭遇後，
那麼快便見到你出來，
真是好啊。」

"Yummy, my favourite," replied Rapunzel.
"It's good to see you out again, so soon after
your terrible ordeal with that nasty wolf."

紅斗篷又再起行將甜餅送去給爸爸吃。
她看看她的籃子，
十個變成九個！

Red Riding Hood set off again to deliver the
freshly made cookies to her Dad.
She looked into her basket.
10 had become 9!

過了一段時間，她來到熊先生和熊太太的家。他們與小熊正在圍坐在花園的桌子，盯著三個空的碗子。
「紅斗篷，紅斗篷，你有食物嗎？我們都很飢餓，有人吃了我們的麥片啊！」

After a while she arrived at Mr and Mrs Bear's house. They were sitting around their garden table with Baby Bear staring into three very empty bowls.
"Red Riding Hood, Red Riding Hood, have you any food? We're starving. Someone's eaten all our porridge!"

紅斗篷是一個善良的女孩，
她將一個新鮮的甜餅放進
每一個碗中。

Now Red Riding Hood was a kind little girl and she popped one freshly
made cookie into each of their bowls.

「啊！謝謝你，」熊先生一家說，「經歷過那次兇惡豺狼的可怕遭遇後，那麼快便見到你出來，真是好啊。」

"Oooooh, thank you," said the bears. "It's good to see you out again, so soon after your terrible ordeal with that nasty wolf."

紅斗篷繼續上路，她看看她的籃子，
九個變成六個！
她走得不遠便來到外婆的家.
「我一定要去看看外婆經歷過那次兇惡豺狼的可怕遭遇後怎麼樣，」
紅斗篷想。

Red Riding Hood marched on. She looked into her basket.
9 had become 6!
She hadn't gone far when she reached Grandma's house.
"I must see how Grandma is after her terrible ordeal with
that nasty wolf," thought Red Riding Hood.

外婆躺在床上。
「外婆，外婆，你好
像很餓，」紅斗篷說。

Grandma was in bed.
"Grandma, Grandma, you look starving," said Red
Riding Hood.

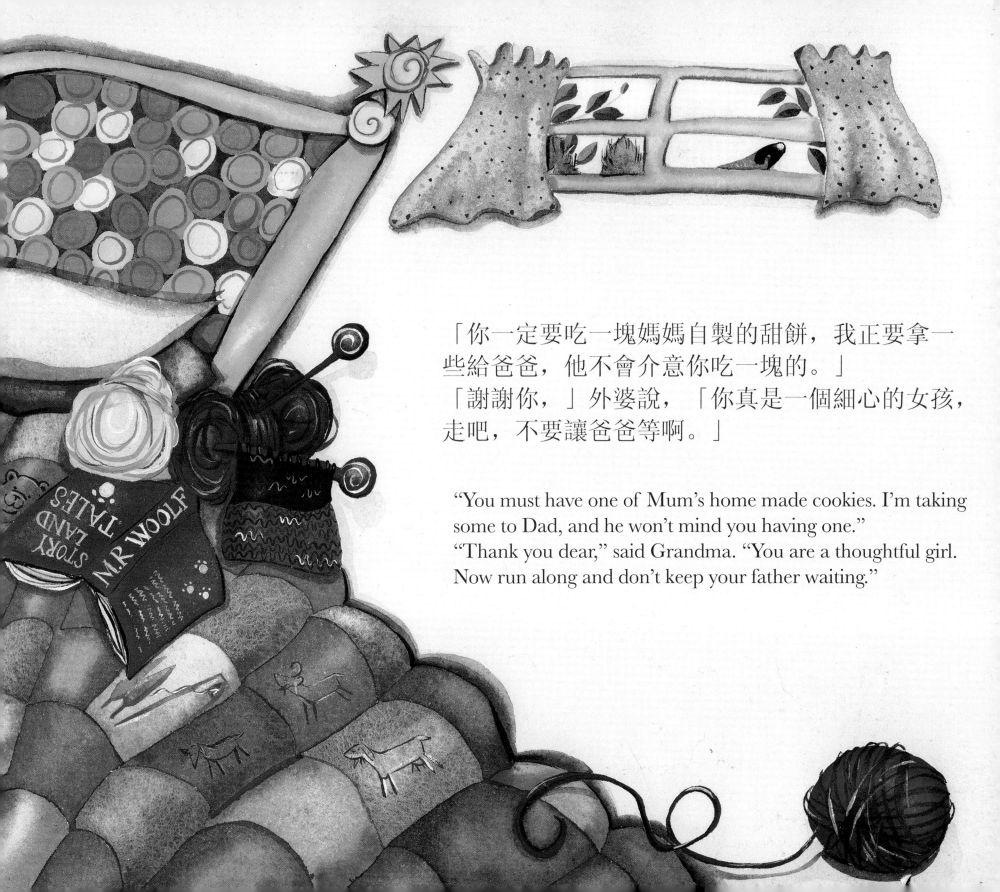

「你一定要吃一塊媽媽自製的甜餅，我正要拿一些給爸爸，他不會介意你吃一塊的。」

「謝謝你，」外婆說，「你真是一個細心的女孩，走吧，不要讓爸爸等啊。」

"You must have one of Mum's home made cookies. I'm taking some to Dad, and he won't mind you having one."

"Thank you dear," said Grandma. "You are a thoughtful girl. Now run along and don't keep your father waiting."

紅斗篷吻外婆的面頰一下後便走去找爸爸。
她看看她的籃子，六個變成五個！

Red Riding Hood gave Grandma a kiss on the cheek
and rushed off to find her Dad.
She looked into her basket. 6 had become 5!

過了一段時間，她走到河邊，三隻瘦骨如
柴的山羊躺在一片枯褐的草地上。
「紅斗篷，紅斗篷，你有食物嗎？
我們都很飢餓。」

After a while she reached the river. Three very scrawny billy goats were lying on a patch of rather brown grass.
"Red Riding Hood, Red Riding Hood, have you any food? We're starving."

「我們不能過橋去吃那邊茂盛的綠草，那裏有一個兇殘飢餓的洞妖等著吃我們。」

"We can't cross the bridge to eat the lush green grass," they said. "There's a mean and hungry troll waiting to eat us."

「你們真可憐啊，吃些甜餅吧，
它們很美味，一，二，三。」

"You poor things, try some home made cookies,
they're delicious. 1, 2, 3."

「你真仁慈啊，」山羊們說，
「經歷過那次兇惡豺狼的可怕遭遇後，
那麼快便見到你出來，真是好啊。」

"You're very kind," said the billy goats. "Nice to see you out again, so soon after your terrible ordeal with that nasty wolf."

紅斗篷繼續上路，她看看她
的籃子，五個變成兩個！
「最低限度這裏周圍沒有飢
餓的豺狼，」紅斗篷想。
就在此時…

Red Riding Hood ran on. She looked into
her basket. 5 had become 2!
"Well at least there aren't any nasty wolves
around here," thought Red Riding Hood.
Just then…

… 一隻豺狼跳到她面前。
「啊，呀，」豺狼說道，「怎麼又是紅斗篷呀，
你經歷過我兄弟的可怕遭遇後，那麼快又出來了。
看到你令我感到有點兒餓。」
「你不能吃我的甜餅，」紅斗篷尖叫道。

...a wolf jumped out in front of her.
"Well, well, well!" said the wolf. "If it isn't Red Riding Hood out again, so soon after
your terrible ordeal with my brother. Seeing you makes me feel rather peckish."
"You can't have any of my cookies," squeaked Red Riding Hood.

「我並不是想吃甜餅啊，」
豺狼一邊吼叫，一邊撲向她。

"I wasn't thinking about cookies,"
growled the wolf as he leapt towards her.

她的爸爸聽到尖叫聲，
揮舞著斧頭出現。

Hearing a scream, her Dad appeared
wielding his axe.

「走啊，紅斗篷，走！」他大聲咆哮，一面趕走豺狼。
「不要又來一次啊！紅斗篷！」爸爸想著。

"Run, Red Riding Hood! Run!" he bellowed as he chased the wolf away.
"Not again, Red Riding Hood," thought Dad.

經歷過這可怕的遭遇後，他們都餓了。
她探手進籃子，「一個給你，一個給我，」
紅斗篷說。

They were both hungry after their terrible ordeal.
She reached into her basket.
"One for you and one for me," said Red Riding Hood.

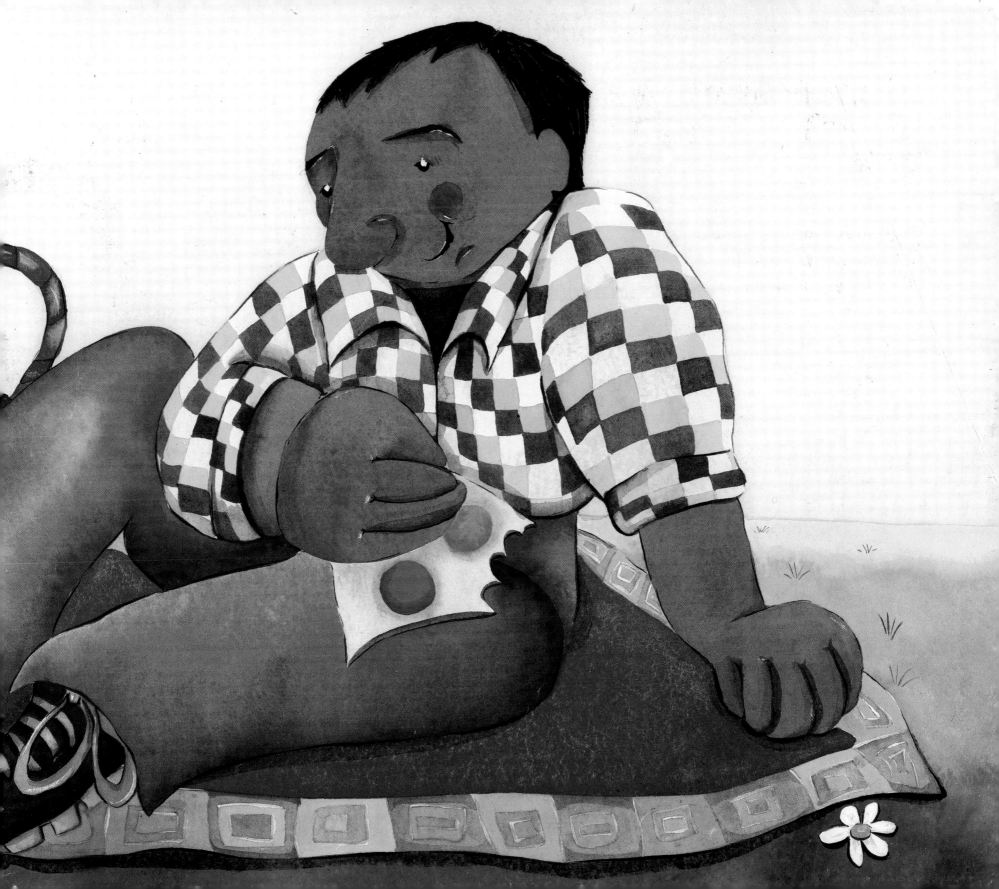

跟著便一個也沒有了。

And then there were none.

British Library Cataloguing-in-Publication Data:
a catalogue record for this book is available
from the British Library.

First published 2003 by Mantra
5 Alexandra Grove, London N12 8NU, UK
www.mantralingua.com